MICHAEL GOW's plays include the Australian classic *Away*, *Toy Symphony*, *The Kid*, *On Top of the World*, *Europe*, *Sweet Phoebe*, *Live Acts on Stage*, *17* (for the Royal National Theatre of Great Britain) and *Once in Royal David's City*. His plays have been performed in Poland, the Czech Republic, Vietnam, Japan and all over the US. Gow has been Associate Director of Sydney Theatre Company and Artistic Director of the Queensland Theatre Company. He has directed for all the major Australian theatre companies as well as Opera Australia, Australian Theatre for Young People and the Lincoln Centre's New Visions New Voices programme. Gow's awards include two NSW Premier's Literary Awards, two Sydney Theatre Critics Circle Awards and an AFI Award for writing the ABC miniseries *Edens Lost*. *Once in Royal David's City* premiered at Belvoir in 2014. In 2015 he directed a remount of his production of *The Magic Flute* for Opera Australia and his translation of *Mother Courage and Her Children* premiered at Belvoir. 2016 saw two critically acclaimed productions touring under Gow's direction with *Voyage to the Moon* (which he also wrote the libretto for) with Victorian Opera / Musica Viva and *The Pearlfishers* for Opera Australia.

ALL STOPS OUT

MICHAEL GOW

CURRENCY PRESS
The performing arts publisher

CURRENCY PLAYS

First published in Australia 1991
by Currency Press Pty Ltd,
PO Box 2287, Strawberry Hills, NSW, 2012, Australia
enquiries@currency.com.au
www.currency.com.au

This edition first published in 2020.

COPYING FOR EDUCATIONAL PURPOSES

The Australian *Copyright Act 1968* (Act) allows a maximum of one chapter or 10% of this book, whichever is the greater, to be copied by any educational institution for its educational purposes provided that that educational institution (or the body that administers it) has given a remuneration notice to Copyright Agency (CA) under the Act.

For details of the CA licence for educational institutions contact CA, 11/66 Goulburn Street, Sydney, NSW, 2000; tel: within Australia 1800 066 844 toll free; outside Australia 61 2 9394 7600; fax: 61 2 9394 7601; email: info@copyright.com.au

COPYING FOR OTHER PURPOSES

Except as permitted under the Act, for example a fair dealing for the purposes of study, research, criticism or review, no part of this book may be reproduced, stored in a retrieval system, or transmitted in any form or by any means without prior written permission. All enquiries should be made to the publisher at the address above.

Any performance or public reading of *All Stops Out* is forbidden unless a licence has been received from the author or the author's agent. The purchase of this book in no way gives the purchaser the right to perform the play in public, whether by means of a staged production or a reading. All applications for public performance should be addressed to the author c/- Shanahan Management, PO Box 1509, Darlinghurst NSW 1300; tel: +61 2 8202 1800.

Typeset by Currency Press.
Cover based on a design by Kate Florance.

Currency Press acknowledges the Traditional Owners of the Country on which we live and work. We pay our respects to all Aboriginal and Torres Strait Islander Elders, past and present.

A catalogue record for this book is available from the National Library of Australia

All Stops Out was first performed by the Australian Theatre for Young People at the Rocks Theatre, Sydney, in July 1989 with the following cast:

SAM	Morgan Lewis
JANE	Virginia Gillard
DANNY	Chris Tomkinson
GRAHAM	Luke Cross
JENNY	Melanie Hickson
LINDA	Toni Collette
CATH	Thomasin Litchfield
IAN	Simon Stokes

Director, Mark Gaal
Designer, Ross Wallace
Lighting designer, Nigel Levings

CHARACTERS

SAM
JANE, his mother
DANNY
GRAHAM, his father
JENNY
LINDA
CATH, a TV journalist
IAN, a cameraman

All the other characters can be doubled or played by different actors, depending on the number of actors available.

SETTING

The action takes place in the homes of Sam and Danny, at work, on the beach and in a committal centre.

PART ONE

SCENE 1

Beach.

DANNY: Who are you?
SAM: My name is Sam.
DANNY: Danny. What are you doing?
SAM: Reading a book.
DANNY: What for?
SAM: I like reading.
DANNY: But this is a beach. What are you reading a book on the beach for? No-one reads books on the beach.
SAM: Lots of people do.
DANNY: Oh yeah, magazines and stuff, crappy books to pass the time, but you're really reading this book, really involved in it, aren't you? How come?
SAM: I've got a lot of reading before school goes back. The HSC this year—
DANNY: You ever been here before?
SAM: No never.
DANNY: Didn't think so. Where you staying?
SAM: In a house near the lagoon.
DANNY: Oh yeah. That's our house up there. With all the glass and shit. We come here all the time, holidays, weekends.
SAM: Big house.
DANNY: Yeah.

GRAHAM, DANNY's father, comes on.

GRAHAM: I want to know if you think you're keeping up your end of the deal? Do you?
DANNY: Oh yeah.
GRAHAM: Definitely not. You've been out all day. You were out all day yesterday, all week. Not a book been opened. You will not get

through this year with good results unless you work. Work hard. I thought that was understood. No?

DANNY: Yeah.

GRAHAM: Don't yeah me.

DANNY: Actually… this is Sam. We're mates. We study together.

GRAHAM: Is that so?

DANNY: Don't we?

SAM: Yes.

DANNY: This is my dad.

GRAHAM: You're on holiday here too?

DANNY: Of course he is.

SAM: Yes I am.

GRAHAM: Which is your house?

SAM: We're staying in a house near the lagoon.

DANNY: We're going to do some study now, aren't we?

SAM: Now?

DANNY: Yeah.

GRAHAM: You doing your HSC this year?

SAM: Yes.

GRAHAM: What are going to do after?

SAM: I'm going to do Arts Law.

GRAHAM: Are you? Good on you.

DANNY: He was reading a book on the beach.

SAM: The novels for English are pretty long, so I thought I'd get them read over the holiday.

GRAHAM: Terrific.

DANNY: Anyway, we'd better get stuck into it.

GRAHAM: You going to stick with Law?

SAM: Yes. I'm going to be a solicitor.

GRAHAM: Or barrister, why not? Sky's the limit.

DANNY: But you have to work, right?

GRAHAM: Your father's footsteps?

SAM: No. My father's an engineer.

GRAHAM: He'll be pleased though.

SAM: Yes he will.

DANNY: Time to work. We're going to Sam's place to read *Romeo and Juliet*.

SAM: No. I have to help Mum getting tea.
DANNY: No. You said we're going to study.
SAM: Not today. Sorry. See ya.

    SAM *goes.*

GRAHAM: You weren't going to study, were you? Have you forgotten we made a deal? You spend the morning on the beach, back for lunch and three hours study in the afternoon.
DANNY: This is a holiday.
GRAHAM: No such thing if you want to get on. I made you promise, all stops out this year. We drew up a timetable, we balanced out reading time, revision time, consolidation time, free time, television time, and we agreed you'd stick to that and in exchange—
DANNY: I could have my holiday mornings to myself, yes.
GRAHAM: We've been here three weeks and you haven't spent more than two hours at your desk. Have you?
DANNY: No.
GRAHAM: Do you understand how serious this year is?
DANNY: Maybe you shouldn't have made me stay at school.
GRAHAM: You're not stupid. You've got it in you, you're lazy, that's all.
DANNY: Maybe I should have done something else.
GRAHAM: Like what? Apprenticeship? To what? Industries that are practically dead.
DANNY: Maybe something else.
GRAHAM: Tell me, Danny, what?
DANNY: I think you should get off my back. We've just finished Christmas.
GRAHAM: When you've got that piece of paper to say you've got a place at university, I'll get off your back.
DANNY: And what'll you do if I don't get that piece of paper? Did you go to university?
GRAHAM: Don't I wish I had.
DANNY: Well, you did something with your life.
GRAHAM: That was twenty years ago. The world's getting narrower every day. Opportunities get smaller. If you don't start off on the right foot, you may as well give it away.

    They go.

SCENE 2

A suburban street.

CATH: Now I'd like you to stand near the fence, is that alright?
IAN: Fine.
CATH: Looks alright?
IAN: Yes, it looks fine.
CATH: And open the letter really slowly, let's see your hands opening it up, then read the results, and then we'll find out how you went, okay.
GIRL: He's coming! Mum, he's coming!

> *A* POSTMAN *approaches the* GIRL.

CATH: Ian, ready?
IAN: Tape's rolling.
POSTMAN: This what you're waiting for?
GIRL: Sure is.
POSTMAN: Good luck

> *The* POSTMAN *goes.*

CATH: Right, good, slowly opening.

> *The* GIRL *reads her results.*

How is it, Kelly?
GIRL: Ummm
CATH: Did what you wanted?
GIRL: No.
CATH: How did you do?
GIRL: Umm… pretty bad. Oh no.
CATH: Did you pass?
GIRL: Passed General Studies. Oh no.
CATH: So how do you feel now, Kelly?
GIRL: What am I going to do? Oh no.
CATH: You're probably feeling really let down now. How do you think your future will be affected?
GIRL: I have to go inside. I have to tell Mum.

CATH: Just one more question. How do you think your parents will accept this disa-ppointment? Follow us, Ian, keep up. Kelly?
GIRL: I'm going inside.

She goes.

CATH: 'In my beginning is my end': ironic words by T.S. Eliot that many of these students have studied. Appropriate for us as we begin this story of the major exam in young people's lives with one possible outcome. Disappointment, confusion... Ian?
IAN: Sorry.
CATH: Why did you stop?
IAN: Pretty awful.
CATH: We agreed when I gave you this job that we'd keep going no matter how upsetting it might appear.
IAN: I know.
CATH: It's part of a much bigger whole. We are here to cover all aspects.
IAN: Yes I know that.
CATH: And you stopped recording.
IAN: She was upset.
CATH: So am I. This isn't a very good start.
IAN: I'll be tougher. From now on.
CATH: Yes?
IAN: It's not that long since I did the exam myself. I felt for her.
CATH: Right. Over it?
IAN: Yes, chief.
CATH: And don't call me chief.

SCENE 3

Committal centre.

LINDA: We don't touch each other's stuff. We don't talk if the other one is lying down or reading a magazine or something. We don't talk after lights out. We do not borrow anything from the other one. We don't even ask for a lend of anything. Making sense?
JENNY: Are these prison rules or just yours?
LINDA: It's how I like things to be. It makes the day easier to get through.

JENNY: Sure.
LINDA: So what did you do?
JENNY: Does it matter?
LINDA: You gotta know who you're stuck with. I don't want to wake up one night with my throat cut or something, a biro embedded in my face.
JENNY: Break and enter.
LINDA: Yeah, you look dumb enough to get caught. First time?
JENNY: First time I got caught. They were able to get me for a few other jobs I'd done. I still had stuff lying around.
LINDA: Really dumb. I'm impressed. Welcome to Paradise.
JENNY: Is this my bed?
LINDA: Bed? Yeah, that's your bed. And the bathroom is in that locker and the jacuzzi's behind that wall and the restaurant has twenty-four-hour room service and the chauffeur is always waiting your every command. Oh, cheer up. This is only day one. Missing anyone?
JENNY: I'm not sure.
LINDA: What's his name.
JENNY: Craig.
LINDA: He sticking by you?
JENNY: Umm…
LINDA: May as well tell me. You'll want to get it off your chest in the end.
JENNY: He kind of got me into this. I don't really know what I think about him just now.
LINDA: He put you up to the job.
JENNY: Yes.
LINDA: Smack?
JENNY: Yes.
LINDA: You use it?
JENNY: A bit.
LINDA: Just to prove you really, really love him and you're his forever. You're not dumb. You're a complete moron. Never catch me doing that for anyone. I don't need anyone that bad. I got myself in here on my own, at least I can say that for myself.
JENNY: What for?
LINDA: Oh, bit of aggro… nothing much really. You see your parents?

JENNY: Yes. Don't you?
LINDA: [*laughing to answer 'no'*] How'd they take this?
JENNY: They're…

She lowers her head as she starts to cry.

LINDA: You play pool?

   JENNY *shakes her head.*

Better learn soon as you can. Need a skill in here.

SCENE 4

Beach.

DANNY: Are you never going to talk to me?
SAM: Yes. This is Danny. This is my mum.
JANE: Hullo.
DANNY: I haven't seen you around for days.
SAM: I've been working.
DANNY: Reading more books?
SAM: That's right.
DANNY: You want to walk around the cliff?
SAM: What for?
DANNY: What for? You always have to have a reason?
SAM: No.
DANNY: Let's go. I'll show you the view.
JANE: Sure, go on.

   They go.

GRAHAM: My son doesn't make friends very easily.
JANE: Neither does mine, Mr…
GRAHAM: Graham.
JANE: Jane.
GRAHAM: You've got a bright boy.
JANE: He does well, but he works hard.
GRAHAM: It's been a good summer. Wonder what the poor people have been doing.
JANE: Their best.
GRAHAM: How long have you had your house here?

JANE: I don't have a house here. I rented it for a few weeks.
GRAHAM: Your husband bring his work here with him?
JANE: My husband?
GRAHAM: He doesn't seem to spend any time on the beach.
JANE: I don't have a husband.
GRAHAM: Sam was saying the other day…
JANE: What was he saying?
GRAHAM: Your husband's an engineer?
JANE: The man who is Sam's father left when Sam was seven. I haven't heard from him since. He could have become an engineer but I really doubt it. What else did Sam tell you? That he goes to a very ordinary government school in the very ordinary suburb we live in? That I have two jobs which leaves me exhausted most of the time. That I have very little money left from either job by the time the rent's paid and the bills are paid and we feed and clothe ourselves, but before this year's school started I spent a little money I'd saved on two weeks rent of a house at the beach. But there was no money left over for the other things you need to come here—surf boards, surfa planes, boogie boards, wind surfers, four-wheel drives, car phones, fax machines and video machines.
GRAHAM: I didn't mean to upset you.
JANE: But you just made the usual assumption that we were here because we had a right to be here with other members of our classless society having a simple beachside holiday. Where your son tries to cover up his embarrassment at his home life by telling cock and bull stories about himself. I'm sorry, I thought I'd left all cares behind on this holiday and they all came up with me in the boot of my unfashionable ten-year-old Ford. I'm sorry, Mr… Graham. Your son. He's doing the HSC?
GRAHAM: Yes. He's not doing all he could, though. It's disappointing.
JANE: Maybe he should be doing something else.
GRAHAM: Such as?
JANE: Hitchhike round the world.
GRAHAM: It's practically the twenty-first century. You think he should go back and live in the nineteen sixties?
JANE: I was only making a suggestion. I hope they both survive the year.
GRAHAM: Now I can see your boy knows exactly where he's going,

what he wants to do with himself. And I see how hard you work to help him get there. Maybe a little too hard. With not much left over when everything's added up.

JANE: Yes.

GRAHAM: I just had this idea that I might help you out a bit, with Sam's education.

JANE: No. Thank you.

GRAHAM: Just provide a few extras.

JANE: I manage.

GRAHAM: I know that, I can see that. You make ends meet.

JANE: Yes I do. And I'll keep making ends meet as long as I have to, so there's no need—

GRAHAM: But if you work all day and half the night you can't see all that much of your boy. Am I right?

JANE: Weekends.

GRAHAM: But you must be worn out.

JANE: Does your wife know you're doing this?

GRAHAM: No. She and I live apart. Do you think your son is getting everything he should to help him through this year? Wouldn't it be better if he had the material things he needs as well as you to support him, encourage him, help him relax when he needs to, and he's going to this year, such a big year. Wouldn't that be a much better way to help him get where he wants?

JANE: And what do you get out of it?

GRAHAM: A bit of pleasure helping someone find success. Not much else.

JANE: I do manage alone.

GRAHAM: I'm not questioning that. But is managing enough? I'll leave you my number.

SCENE 5

Cliff.

SAM: It's high.
DANNY: Scared?
SAM: Umm, no.

DANNY: Sure?
SAM: I'm not scared.
DANNY: We just have to get to that ledge. Keep going.
SAM: I'm not scared.
DANNY: Made it, see. Keep going.
SAM: I'm alright!
DANNY: Good view, eh?
SAM: What of?
DANNY: The sea. When the tide's right in and there's a swell, the spray reaches right up here.

> DANNY *reaches into a crevice and takes out a bottle of Scotch.*

Here.
SAM: What is it?
DANNY: Black Douglas. Eight years old before they sell it. Go on.
SAM: No thanks.
DANNY: Why not?
SAM: I don't drink Black Douglas.
DANNY: I used to have Johnny Walker but it ran out. Go on, have a swig.
SAM: No.
DANNY: Yeah, go on, part of the thrill, climbing up here. Two kids been killed climbing on this cliff. Straight down. What a mess. Couldn't get to them for hours.

> SAM *takes a swig of Scotch.*

You like it here?
SAM: I think I should go back now.
DANNY: No, I mean up here for a holiday.
SAM: Yeah, it's okay. Lot of rich people here.
DANNY: Deadshits. You like school?
SAM: Oh yeah.
DANNY: Must be great being a brain. Make everything so much easier. I hate school. I really hate it. I don't want to be there. Dad makes me. He wants me to get into university. He wants me to get a really great job. But I'm stupid. So I'm wasting my time. You're going to do really well in the exams. I can tell. Your old man'll be really pleased.

SAM: I haven't got an old man. My father walked out on Mum when I was really little. I can hardly remember him.
DANNY: Yeah?
SAM: My mother has two jobs.
DANNY: I wasn't the only one lying the other day.
SAM: No.
DANNY: I really got an earful after you went.
SAM: I'm sorry I didn't go along with it.
DANNY: You had it in for me.
SAM: I thought you really wanted to talk. But you just used me to stay out of the shit with your dad.
DANNY: I'm sorry. You don't hate me?
SAM: Nup.
DANNY: I thought you were a joke at first, sitting on the beach reading a book. When I saw my old man coming along the beach looking for me I freaked. Have another drink.
SAM: I should go back now.
DANNY: One more drink.

    SAM *has another drink.*

Does your mother make you study all the time?
SAM: No. I just do it.
DANNY: So you really want to be a lawyer?
SAM: Yeah. I s'pose.
DANNY: I miss my mother. She and Dad split up and she thought I'd do better at school if I stayed with Dad. She's in Europe or somewhere. She wouldn't have made me stay at school. [*Pause.*] What are you doing tomorrow?
SAM: We have to pack up tomorrow. We're going home.
DANNY: Right. Listen. How about we study anyway. I hate studying by myself, I can't really do it. What do you say? Couple of times a week or something. You provide the brain and I'll provide the Black Douglas and chips and stuff. We got off to a lousy start, but we could get through the year a bit easier maybe. Yeah?
SAM: So your father'll lay off?
DANNY: No. I need help and you need…
SAM: What?

DANNY: You need a mate. I'll write my number down before you go.
SAM: Yeah.
DANNY: Yeah?
SAM: We'll get together. See ya. Good luck.
DANNY: Hey, Sam.
SAM: What?
DANNY: Don't look down.

SCENE 6

Schoolyard.

CATH: So how do you feel about your first day back?
KIDS: Ohhhhh.
CATH: You pleased to be back?
KIDS: Naaaaaaaaaa.
CATH: You going to work hard this year?
KIDS: Yeeeeeeeeeeeeeah.
CATH: You all doing the HSC?
KIDS: Errrrrrrrrrrrrrrrr.
CATH: You all going to pass?
KIDS: Ooooooooooh... dunnoooooooo.
CATH: You all like school?
KIDS: Naaaaaaaaaaaaaaaah.
ONE KID: I do.
KIDS: Dickhead. Jerk. Dag. Shut uuuuuuuuuuup.
CATH: So what do you think of the year ahead?
KIDS: Yuuuuuuuuuuuuuuuuuuuuuk.

SCENE 7

Sam's place.

A)

JANE: Can I interrupt?
SAM: You're not interrupting.

JANE: History?
SAM: Russian Revolution.
JANE: Something very serious has happened. I've been sacked from my night job. The company's been going downhill for a while and they just got rid of fifty of us last night. It's going to get really hard now. I don't know what to do.
SAM: Don't worry, we'll be fine.
JANE: Will we?
SAM: Sure. We'll scrape through. I'll pass my exams with flying colours and before you know it I'll have a highly-paid job and we'll move to a flat overlooking the harbour and you can ditch the other job as well. Then when I'm married to a really nice young woman we'll move to a large house to have our kids and you can have the flat to yourself except when you babysit the kids while we take our overseas holidays. Everything will be okay.
JANE: Good. Good boy. Now back to work.

B)

JANE: [*nervous, restless, barely listening to* SAM] Can I interrupt?
SAM: You're not interrupting.
JANE: History?
SAM: Russian Revolution.
JANE: I've been thinking about a few things, Sam. It's been worrying me I don't spend enough time with you, enough time around the place. This is such a big year.
SAM: We do okay.
JANE: But the closer we get to exam time the more support you're going to need.
SAM: I get that.
JANE: I feel it's important for me to be here when you might need me.
SAM: You always are.
JANE: When the stress gets too great it's very important to any student to have an escape valve.
SAM: You do everything you could.
JANE: So I've decided to give up the evening job. We'll manage very easily, you've got everything you'll need for the year, so what's the

point of holding down two jobs when I could be here helping you? Getting you through this year is the most important thing. Once the year is over, I'll think again, but for the moment everything else can take a back seat to you and the exam.

SAM: So you just stopped?

JANE: I gave him a week's notice. Oh, it'll be good to be home at night. No more buses in the cold, no more fighting through the traffic from one job to the other. Just us, getting through the year.

SCENE 8

Committal centre.

LINDA: Have you met Sandra yet?

JENNY: Ahhh, yes. She the one with the glass eye?

LINDA: That's her. She's amazing. Talk about guts. She'd stand up to a rhinoceros, I reckon. And have you run into Margot? She's in for assault. Great chick. S'pose if you're that big you're not afraid of anyone. Have you seen the way she eats? Shovels it in.

JENNY: Mm.

LINDA: So don't you talk?

JENNY: I talk.

LINDA: What's so good about the book?

JENNY: Nothing.

LINDA: What is it?

JENNY: Linda, isn't there a rule about when someone's reading or lying down the other one isn't supposed to talk?

LINDA: Yeah, but… magazines and stuff.

JENNY: I'm reading.

LINDA: It's a book. What sort of book?

JENNY: Science textbook.

LINDA: Science textbook! Yuuuk. Where did you get that?

JENNY: Oh, out of the library.

LINDA: Bull. Did that social worker give it to you?

JENNY: Yes she did.

LINDA: She's a pain in the arse. She should be out saving starving people in the jungle or somewhere. She's so good. We call her The

Saint. Why did she give it to you? Are you a brain or something?
JENNY: No I'm not a brain. She looked up my records and found out I never finished school. I dropped out after I first met Craig and never did the HSC. She thought maybe I could do it while I'm in here.
LINDA: What for?
JENNY: Good way to spend the time. Better than sitting around doing nothing, she thinks.
LINDA: That what you think?
JENNY: Maybe.
LINDA: So what are you reading about?
JENNY: The Mohorovocik discontinuity.
LINDA: Is that a disease?
JENNY: It's where the earth's crust and mantle meet.
LINDA: Waste of time, don't you reckon?
JENNY: Is it?
LINDA: It is. Total waste of time. School. All that. What good will it do you?
JENNY: I don't know.
LINDA: No good at all. Teachers! School! Makes me sick. I mean everything's stuffed, don't you reckon. The government, the world, everything. It's all going down the drain. And why? Because of all the brainy people in the world who've stuffed it all up. Like, it's people with educations who've put us in here. People who think they know all the answers because they went to uni. Big deal, uni. And all the wars. And nuclear bombs. And pollution. All because brainy people were allowed to do what they thought was best. Right?
JENNY: I s'pose.
LINDA: Yeah. That's where ninety-nine percent of the world's problems come from. Too many people with educations who are stuffing everybody and everything right up. I got no time for them. So don't you let me catch you reading that stuff again. That's a serious warning, okay? I don't want to see that stuff in here again. Or else.

SCENE 9

Graham's office.

JANE: I feel like I'm in a film, coming to see you in secret like this.

GRAHAM: Not a secret, is it?

JANE: I haven't told Sam I've come to see you. I'd rather you didn't tell Danny.

GRAHAM: No need to.

JANE: I lost my night job. Things weren't going well for the company and they had to lay off quite a few people. There was a minute when I was actually pleased I didn't have to go there anymore. I hated it. It was so noisy. But it's going to leave a big hole in my finances. I'm really going to miss it.

GRAHAM: You need some money now?

JANE: No, it's not desperate, but in a few months I'm going to really notice it. There are some big bills coming in, Christmas to pay off, it'll be Sam's birthday soon and then some new winter clothes. I can't take it out of what we normally live on because I don't want Sam's routine upset. And I don't want him to be worrying about any of this.

GRAHAM: You didn't tell him you lost the job.

JANE: I told him I gave it up to spend more time with him, help him. I sounded like a personal growth workshop, the junk I was coming out with. But I didn't tell him, no.

GRAHAM: You don't want a loan?

JANE: I want to know… This is so hard to ask. I know I can get through this, I know I can be independent, I'm not a failure at what I'm trying to do—

GRAHAM: Of course you're not.

JANE: But I'll do anything to make sure Sam gets through the HSC. If I need to ask, if it gets to that point, will you help? Only if it gets desperate, only then.

GRAHAM: Sure.

JANE: It won't be much, just to stay ahead of bills and anything Sam might need that will come up.

GRAHAM: Whatever you need. Just ask, if and when the time comes.
JANE: And I'll keep a full account of everything. It would only be a loan.
GRAHAM: Whatever you like.
JANE: You won't tell Danny?
GRAHAM: What would be the point?
JANE: I feel like a spy making a secret contact. Thank you.

SCENE 10

Suburban lounge room.

PARENT: Now the thing is, right, we don't feel our kiddies are being fairly treated, right? Now it's all very well to encourage these people to try and fit in here, right—
CATH: Which people is that?
PARENT: You know, Asians'n that. It's all very well to encourage them to fit in and that, although they shouldn't be allowed to talk their own lingo, but it's going too far letting them do the same exam as Australian kiddies.
IAN: They are Australian.
CATH: Shhhh. They are Australian surely.
IAN: [*under his breath*] What?
CATH: Ian...
PARENT: You see they don't have the same attitude to things as we do. Their homes for instance. They're much happier living crammed into a couple of rooms, well it's what they're used to I s'pose, but they don't have the same need for privacy and a little bit of room as Australians. It's the same with the way they study. Now they don't treat school the way an Australian kiddie does. An Australian kiddie will do his homework and a little bit of study and then he'll go out and play a little bit of sport, watch a little bit of tele, something to relax. But some of these Asian kiddies, they're obsessed. They work day and night. They never rest. All they do is study and read, read and study, all the time. That's the way they are. They cram it in non-stop. Well, if that's the case they really should do a different exam from our kiddies, to make it more fair.

IAN: This is crazy.
CATH: Ah… Well, thank you very much for your opinion. [*To the camera*] Another angle on the always controversial education debate.
PARENT: And it goes on right through the universities and colleges too. They don't do anything but study. That's why they get all the jobs.
IAN: Maybe they're just more intelligent.
PARENT: No fear! They have different shaped brains!
IAN: We're finished. You can turn him [*or her*] off now.
CATH: We have to cover all aspects. It's a very big topic.
IAN: Too big for lunatics.
CATH: A lot of people think like that.
IAN: God help us.
CATH: Who's doing this probe?
PARENT: But you'd never get me going to a doctor or a butcher called Mr Ling or Mr Tran Ban Ngong. No fear. You put that on your television program.

SCENE 11

Sam's place.

DANNY: So the theme is the abstract central idea.
SAM: The plot?
DANNY: Is the story which illustrates the theme. The story.
SAM: Yes.
DANNY: So why not call it the story? Plot, sounds like someone planning something in secret, let's drive all school kids crazy, let's start a plot that says everything they read is impossible to understand.
SAM: So the theme of *Romeo and Juliet* is…
DANNY: Um… the destructive power of passion.
SAM: And the plot…
DANNY: … is the drama of two innocents who meet by accident and… and are destroyed by forces they can't deal with. Could be about us.
SAM: What about imagery? What's a metaphor?
DANNY: When you make a comparison between two things identifying one with the other. Like 'It is the east and Juliet is the sun'.

SAM: And what's a simile?
DANNY: Same thing only you use like or as. This is all just... stuff. If I remember all this, and use it to answer questions, that means I'm educated? Once the exam's over I can forget it all and it won't have meant a thing.
SAM: S'pose.
DANNY: And you're good at school because you can remember all this.
SAM: No, I'm good at school because I can be bothered remembering all this. Anyone can remember junk like this. You see... that's why I do these subjects—English, History, all that. You just remember all these things, then mix them all around and mention everything you know and throw in a few examples and that's it. Remember when you first said you hate school? I despise school. It just gets in the way. That book I was reading on the beach that day, that had nothing to do with school. It was a book by someone I read about in a book about the novel we're supposed to study. I hate the stuff we're supposed to read, there's so much to read that's better, more interesting, more exciting, I keep reading that. I have to force myself to read these books. Whenever we're supposed to read *Romeo and Juliet*, that's when I want to read Jane Austen. When we're supposed to read Andrew Marvell I want to read Isaac Asimov. Have you read *Foundation and Empire*? It's great. Whenever we're supposed to read Keats I want to read *Jude the Obscure*. I love reading but I hate school. It's torture. But I have to do it. If only I was free to just read whatever I wanted, just get lost in books and writers and ideas. But you have to come back to the theme of *Romeo and Juliet* and character in the modern novel and compare and contrast Andrew Marvell and... and a two-headed cow. I'm no good helping you. I'm a fraud, Danny. I don't even want to do Law. God, what am I saying? I'm doing it for my mother. Every time she looks in on me with my desk lamp on and all the books stacked around the desk, I can feel her wanting me to be a genius, to get five hundred and one out five hundred and become the world's greatest lawyer. All I want to do is read a book about something that's not on the course. I'm a fraud.
DANNY: Drink?
SAM: What would be really great would be if they just said read fifty

books and see fifty films and go to ten foreign countries and learn ten poems and join a rock group and come back in two years and we'll give you the Higher School Certificate.

DANNY: Or get a job and start making money when you turn fifteen and we'll help you learn what you need to know. That would be excellent.

SAM: But we're stuck with this stuff. Cram it in and forget it two days after the exam. Oh, let me out of here. I need some air.

DANNY: Have at thee coward.

SAM: Hence, knave, avaunt thee, outside to thy bike.

SCENE 12

Committal centre.

LINDA: How come you disappeared?

JENNY: Felt tired.

LINDA: The game was getting really interesting.

JENNY: Wanted to lie down.

LINDA: Don't you like pool?

JENNY: Yes. It's a good game.

LINDA: So why didn't you stay and watch? You aren't going to learn sitting in here all the time.

JENNY: I felt homesick.

LINDA: You didn't watch the game Tuesday either. You tired then?

JENNY: I wanted to write a letter.

LINDA: To your beloved?

JENNY: Mum and Dad.

LINDA: But you shouldn't just walk out in the middle of a game like that.

JENNY: Sorry.

LINDA: This place is full of very suspicious people, you know. They might start to worry. They might get a bit edgy.

JENNY: I'll make sure it doesn't—

LINDA: Might think you're doing something secret, that you don't want anyone else to know about.

JENNY: Like what?

LINDA: Like reading that book you've stuffed under the mattress. Give it to me.

JENNY: I just picked it up when I came back to lie down.

LINDA: Give it to me.

JENNY: It doesn't really interest me. You're right about everything being stuffed. I mean what's the point of studying and stuff like that? I mean there isn't any, is there?

LINDA: Didn't I tell you I didn't want to see this stuff in here ever again?

JENNY: Yes.

LINDA: So what's it doing here?

JENNY: I was reading it.

LINDA: Were you?

JENNY: The social worker's arranging for me to sit the exam. I thought I may as well do it.

LINDA: I don't think that's really such a good idea. I think The Saint is just sticking her nose in where it's not really wanted. Don't you reckon?

JENNY: Yeah.

LINDA: So maybe you should tell her you're not really all that interested in doing this HSC. She'll understand. Social workers are very understanding people. When are you seeing her again?

JENNY: She's coming in at the end of the week.

LINDA: You can tell her then. Can't you?

JENNY: Yes.

LINDA: Good. Got that cleared up really well, didn't we. We can go back to the game now. And we can drop this useless book off at the incinerator on the way there.

JENNY: What are you afraid of?

LINDA: Who's afraid?

JENNY: Are you afraid of books? The very first time you saw this textbook you went a bit pale. Do they frighten you?

LINDA: No.

JENNY: Why won't you let me study?

LINDA: I don't want you wasting your time.

JENNY: That's not a reason. You are afraid.

LINDA: I'm not.

JENNY: You're afraid I might end up a bit intelligent.
LINDA: Bull.
JENNY: Here. Look inside the book. Is that what makes you so upset? A few diagrams? Bit of writing?
LINDA: I'm going to the rec room.
JENNY: You're afraid. That's why you're trying to stand over me. I bet everyone who comes near you has to stay the way they are or else you get frightened. You're terrified I won't end up like you.
LINDA: You already have. You're in here. But I'll get out again.
JENNY: Yeah, and you'll end up straight back in again, everyone does. Once you walk through the door of a place like this you can bet you'll never leave.
JENNY: I will.
LINDA: Forget it.
JENNY: I'll try.
LINDA: What for?
JENNY: Because.
LINDA: Moron.
JENNY: I'm not a moron. And I'm not going to try and become one, like you. This stuff is interesting. I can't stop myself from being interested. So I'm going to read it. Right? Even if it gets me nowhere, I'm going to read it. Right?

Silence.

Right?
LINDA: Do what you like.
JENNY: I will.
LINDA: Good.
JENNY: So leave me alone. I'm going to study.
LINDA: Great.
JENNY: Now.
LINDA: Good on you.

SCENE 13

Office of a concerned parent.

CATH: What exactly do you have against the books you've complained about?

PARENT: It's like this. These books that are being pushed onto our children. Now they aren't what you'd call normal books. They do not contain the sort of reading matter that young folk should in all seriousness be reading. They do not contain uplifting material, the stories do not present suitable role models for young people to follow, they present disturbing themes, distorted views of human relationships, morbid ideas, constant use of foul language, and an overexaggerated stressing of sexual matters.

CATH: You advocate banning of books?

PARENT: Not in so many words, no, no, no. My goodness that would be totalitarian, and we do not advocate totalitarian tactics. But we do insist on the right to keep a control over what our young people, future citizens, are reading. Young people have no understanding of the major questions of life. They know nothing as yet of the terrible problems and tensions that beset adult life. There is no need to expose them to these troubling and often deeply disturbing views of human life. What do sixteen-year-olds know of fear, anxiety, feelings of dread and the nightmares that some of these so-called avant-garde writers that they are being forced to read put forward?

IAN: You don't know?

CATH: Shh.

PARENT: What?

CATH: Nothing.

IAN: Must be blind.

CATH: Ian. I'm sorry. Some of the books you are questioning are considered great classics of literature.

PARENT: Depends on what you call a classic really. A classic is something that speaks of the greatness of the human spirit, a classic uplifts, comforts, celebrates achievement. There are plenty of books available to our so-called educators that pass this test.

IAN: The Secret Seven.
CATH: Look…
PARENT: Is there something the…
CATH: No, it's a technical… That's covered your basic position I think.
PARENT: If you think that's alright.
CATH: It's very good.
PARENT: Marvellous.
CATH: Thank you.

The PARENT *goes.*

IAN: Basic position is their heads up their bums.
CATH: Are you secretly working for another network?
IAN: No.
CATH: I get the feeling you'd like this program to turn out a mess.
IAN: That's not true.
CATH: Why are you sabotaging what I'm trying to do?
IAN: What are you trying to do?
CATH: Present a picture of the world of education, the problems people face coming to terms with the HSC, its role as the final rite of passage in the lives—
IAN: You should stick to the lives of the people doing the exam. Not those dried-up old mummies.
CATH: Their opinions are quite widely held.
IAN: Then there's no need to advertise them anymore. Those people! God, how out of touch can you get?
CATH: If you're not happy with this project I can easily find someone else.
IAN: Do you agree with them?
CATH: No, not really—
IAN: But you just threatened me with the sack unless I keep my opinions to myself.
CATH: It's different.
IAN: Bull. Just because you're the TV personality and I'm crew you get to have opinions and I don't? Is that the way it is?
CATH: Well… no. But…
IAN: What?
CATH: It makes it that much more difficult to do the project.

IAN: So? It's not easy doing the HSC, why should we sell them all short and promote dickheads like those people? Just to get a bit of controversy in the viewing, so a lot of terrified parents can feel better if there's someone on TV saying the world's going to the dogs because kids are too intelligent and should be made dumber. If that's the sort of show you want to do then fine, I'll go back to filming car accidents and stupid people missing at sea. Yes?

CATH: But if we're going to turn everything into an issue we won't get anything done.

IAN: Everything is an issue. Before I did this I worked on this drug report that was full of shock horror stuff to get the dickheads going. And all the crew, all the office staff and the reporter were stoned the whole time. I remember those exams. I reckon my brain still has the scars. I think we can do better. What's wrong with a bit of healthy argument, anyway, chief?

CATH: Don't call—

IAN: Sorry, boss.

CATH: I'm not your…

IAN: Where next? Parliament House?

SCENE 14

Graham's office.

GRAHAM: We could have lunch.

JANE: No.

GRAHAM: I hate seeing you in this office all the time.

JANE: No, I don't feel like sitting in a crowded restaurant.

GRAHAM: Takeaway in the park?

JANE: I'm sorry, I… The rent's gone up. Twenty dollars a week.

GRAHAM: That must make a big difference.

JANE: It's only a question of what to do without. I don't think eating lunch anywhere would seem right at the moment.

GRAHAM: On me.

JANE: No, I'll accept money if it directly affects Sam.

GRAHAM: And the rent does?

JANE: There are a couple of excursions he wants to go on and he's always wanting books, to read for himself or to help with his work. I can't say no to them, can I?

GRAHAM: No.

JANE: So that's what you'd be helping with. That's all.

GRAHAM: Sure.

JANE: Thank you for offering lunch. I really wish I could just say yes and relax for an hour or two.

GRAHAM: Isn't there anything you'd like to do? For yourself? A movie? Dinner? You can't go on week after week without thinking of your own sanity a few times

JANE: There's a hell of a lot of things I'd like to do, believe me. But I can't have them if I go into debt. And I don't just mean financial debt.

GRAHAM: Maybe you should stop seeing everything in terms of debt, loan, paying back. If something's offered to you, accept it.

JANE: It's been a hard fight to get where I am.

GRAHAM: I know, I know.

JANE: If I start accepting everything that's offered, even from a friend, where does that leave all the time up till now? Years I've spent staying independent. Does this mean I can't? I can't have the best for Sam and stay my own boss? Sounds like a big defeat to me. A big failure. My son passes his exams and I fail parenthood.

GRAHAM: At least you see me as a friend. That's something positive.

JANE: I wasn't sure about your offer. But I haven't found any strings. Yet.

GRAHAM: And you won't. I'll sign this cheque, you fill in what you need. Any amount.

JANE: No. Look I made a list, added it up roughly—

GRAHAM: If I'm going to do this for you at least I want to feel a bit human, not an automatic teller. Here.

JANE: Thank you. You know, as soon as I—

GRAHAM: I know. And I believe you. What are you doing after school finishes for the year?

JANE: I don't know. Nothing.

GRAHAM: Come up to the beach. Wait for the results. Four of us could have a reasonably relaxing time after the madness. You keep talking

about paying this back. Fine. But a holiday can be the interest on the loan.
JANE: I'll think about it.
GRAHAM: It'd do you a lot of good. You'll need it after getting through the year.
JANE: We all will. The boys seem to be studying well.
GRAHAM: I can't believe how much Danny's improved. He wants me to send him to a lecture series at one of the universities, for kids doing the HSC. I can't believe it.
JANE: Sam mentioned those.
GRAHAM: He want to go?
JANE: He thinks he should.
GRAHAM: You've got the cheque.
JANE: I'll call you in a few weeks.

END OF PART ONE

PART TWO

SCENE 15

Theatre.

JASON 1: Hey, Jase, where's the chips?
JASON 2: I ate them.
JASON 1: You ate them?
JASON 2: Yeah.
KYLIE 1: Shhh.
JASON 1: Who said that?
JASON 3: That chick over there.
JASON 1: Hey, beautiful!
KYLIE 1: Shhhh.
JASON 1: Wanna go out after this is finished?
KYLIE 2: Ignore him, Kylie.
JASON 2: She's ignoring you, Jason.
JASON 1: Mole.
JASON 2: They're starting up again.
ACTOR: Eyes, look your last. Arms, take your last embrace! And lips, O you the doors of breath, seal with a righteous kiss A dateless bargain to engrossing death!—

Romeo kisses Juliet.

ALL KIDS: Ohhhhhhhhhhhhhhhhhhhhhhh.
JASON 3: Put your tongue in!
JASON 2: Have a look up her dress!
KYLIE 2: Shhhh.
ACTOR: Come, bitter conduct, come, unsavoury guide!
JASON 1: Reckon he's gonna come!
KYLIE 2: Oh, look you boys, shut upl
JASON 1: Bet you wish it was you up there under him.
KYLIE 1: Well, he's spunkier than you.
KYLIE 3: Hey, Kylie, do you know if he's been in *Neighbours*?
JASON 1: Reckon he's been in Juliet.

PART TWO

KYLIE 2: Shhh, this is the sad bit.
ACTOR: [*struggling on*]
   Thou desperate pilot, now at once run on
   The dashing rocks thy sea-sick weary barque!
BOYS: Woof, woof, woof, aroo!
ACTOR: That's it. I've had it. I'm up here working my arse off for you morons and all you can do is behave like… morons.

The KIDS *all make mock amazed noises.*

Well, you can all get stuffed.

The KIDS *all make mock shocked noises.*

Go home and watch soap opera. More your level. I don't have to put up with this. Come on, Angela, let's get out of here.

He leaves the stage.

KIDS: Angela?!

The ACTRESS *turns and raises her middle fingers to the* KIDS *then storms off. The* KIDS *applaud and whistle.*

KYLIE 2: Satisfied?
JASON 1: Not yet, sweetheart.
KYLIE 1: No, Kylie, I reckon he's in *Home and Away*.
JASON 2: Is that it?
JASON 1: Yeah, let's get out of here.
JASON 3: What'll we do now, Jason?
JASON 2: Let's throw cans in the harbour.
JASON 3: No, let's ride around on the trains for a while.
JASON 1: You wanna come for a ride?
KYLIE 2: No we don't.
KYLIE 1: No, we're gonna wait and see if it is the guy out of *Neighbours*.
JASON 1: Shakespeare sucks, eh Jase?
KYLIE 2: Yeah, well when you do your exam you won't know how the play ends, will you?
JASON 1: Yeah.
KYLIE 2: You're too stupid to be able to read. You've had it.
JASON 1: Who's stupid?
GIRLS: You are!

SCENE 16

Outside a country homestead.

CATH: You feel you're disadvantaged by living out here on a station?
KID: Ohhhh... no.
CATH: But living so far from the city might make you feel a bit out of touch with the mainstream of the education system?
KID: Ohhhhh... no.
CATH: Do the subjects you have to study have any relevance to life on a sheep station?
KID: Ohhhhh... yeah.
CATH: But I would have thought studying for the HSC would have little to do with the practical day-to-day, hands-on work of running a place like this.
KID: Ohhhhh... sorry?
CATH: Ummm. What subjects are you studying?
KID: Well... Advanced Shearing. Three-Unit Sheep Dip. Applied Dagging and ... Castration.

IAN can't contain his laughter anymore.

IAN: Sorry. I'm sorry.
CATH: Did you cook this up?
IAN: Sorry.
CATH: We drove all the way out here so you could have a little joke. That's it. You're off this project. And I suppose you think you're really funny as well. I'm going to find a real student to talk to. On my own. You two can go to the pub where you belong.
KID: I am a real student. I'm sitting the HSC this year.
CATH: Sure.
KID: It's true. I'm doing English, Rural Tech and Biology and Maths. I know how to build a house, fix a tractor, write a full scientific report on the soil of this district, do spreadsheets for a large station with subsidiary businesses. I can do wages breakdowns for a full complement of shearers and staff and for my personal interest project I'm studying the salination of the land on our property and ways of reversing it. What can you do?

He goes. CATH *can't think of anything to say.*

IAN: Drink, boss?
CATH: I'll wait in the car.

SCENE 17

Sam's place.

DANNY: The maths is still hard, but I'm working on it. I enrolled in that study day at the university. You?
SAM: No.
DANNY: I thought we were going to go together.
SAM: I'm not going.
DANNY: Great day out.
SAM: I'm not going.
DANNY: The English stuff is so easy. Got all the themes of all the poems down. I can name fifteen metaphors. I learnt ona… ona… mata… peoia last night. Pow. Bang. Clink. So easy! I haven't read Mansfield Park. Now that is hard. But I asked the teacher. She's actually helping me to read it. Then I rattle off what I think might be the theme of the book and she looks at me like this—really impressed!
SAM: You want a drink?
DANNY: Sorry, I didn't bring anything.
SAM: I've got my own bottle. I keep it hidden behind the ancient history notes.
DANNY: The theme of *The Trojan Women* is the suffering caused by war or man's inhumanity to man, I can't remember. I've brought your notes on the Egyptians back. Did all the stuff they put in the tombs with the farouts.
SAM: The what?
DANNY: That's how I remember 'pharaoh'. The Egyptians were ruled by men who were 'farout'… pharaoh. The colours of the spectrum are Mr Roy G. Biv. Red: orange, yellow, green—
SAM: I can't do any study tonight. I can't do any study at all. What am I going to do? The minute I knew I was doing it so easily I knew it didn't mean anything. I'm wasting my time. Every time I sit down

to revise, or read, that's what I think—I'm wasting my time. I can't do it anymore.
DANNY: You handing in essays and junk?
SAM: They get later and later. The only thing that makes me get them in on time at all is the thought that one of the teachers will ask Mum if there's anything wrong. I wish I was learning because I really wanted to learn! Then I could get going again.
DANNY: But it's just a game. That's how I'm doing it. Don't take it so seriously. That's why it's such a big problem. It's just a game. Dad can't believe it. He just keeps checking on me and saying, 'Sure you're not working too hard?' And I just open another book and he leaves me alone again. It's great!
SAM: A game.
DANNY: Yep.
SAM: Let's stop this. Let's watch TV.
DANNY: No. You don't want to work?
SAM: No.
DANNY: Sure?
SAM: Yes.
DANNY: I might go then. I want to do some maths. It's the only really tough stuff. I'm getting there though.

SCENE 18

Committal centre.

LINDA: It won't interest you, but I won the tournament.
JENNY: Mm.
LINDA: Yeah. [*Pause.*] So you're never going to speak to me again, right? That's fine. I can take it. No problem. I'm getting on real well not speaking to anyone in my own room. It's easy. Like I said that day, I don't need anyone.
JENNY: What day?
LINDA: The day you said I… I'm a moron.
JENNY: Takes one to know one.
LINDA: So you're really busy right now?
JENNY: Just revising this stuff about continental drift.

PART TWO

LINDA: What a joke.
JENNY: So I'm pretty busy.
LINDA: What's continental drift?
JENNY: There's this theory that all the continents were once joined up. See if you put them all together in a certain way, they fit. Like a jigsaw puzzle.
LINDA: Hey, yeah.
JENNY: And once there was just one big land mass called... Pangaea. I'm trying to memorise the spelling. They're really weird words, some of them. See if I'm right.
LINDA: Ahhh, no thanks. You can manage on your own. Smart kid doesn't need a moron to help her get by.
JENNY: Just see if I've got it right. P.A.N.G.E.A.E.
LINDA: Nup. P.A.N.G.A.E.A.
JENNY: Right. A.E.A.—P.A.N.G.A.E.A.
LINDA: That's it.
JENNY: And the sea was called... Tethys. T.E.T.H.Y.S. Right?
LINDA: Yep. Where was the Pacific? I've heard of that because the boyfriend Mum had before the last one took her on a cruise around the Pacific. She sent me this postcard. She didn't take me because she said I'd only be bored and I can be a real little creep when I'm bored. So she says.
JENNY: Are you?
LINDA: S'pose I am. If you're bored what else is there to do? Wouldn't have mattered, they split up after six months. I went to live with my father for a little while because Mum wanted to be on her own but he was travelling a lot and Mum thought he'd take off with me and he couldn't get a different job—well you know how hard it is to get a job—so I went back to her and the new guy she was with said I was uncontrollable or maybe I was mentally disturbed, but he used to come into my room at night, you know, and want to fool around and, God, it's not on, so I'd scream at him and in the end he chucked me out so I was hanging out on the street for a while and we started stealing cars, just to sleep in on cold nights, that's all, and then this nightwatchman caught us and one of the boys thumped him... and we got caught... and...

She finds herself in tears.

JENNY: So they're not really sure what was there before all these continents started drifting around, but they know what happened after. Pangaea split into two, Laurasia and Gondwanaland. Isn't that a great name? Gondwanaland. Australia was part of Gondwanaland. There are fossil records of things that lived in places that now are thousands and thousands of miles away from each other. That's one of the things that made them think of this theory. I'm doing fossils as well. You ever seen a fossil?

LINDA: No.

JENNY: When the animal died it got covered with layers of mud and over the years it turned to stone and then they were dug up and we know what animals looked like even though they haven't been around for millions of years. That's what's so great about this stuff. If things like dinosaurs can disappear—and they were huge and really mean... well, nothing could be as frightening, that's where the word dinosaur comes from, it means thunder lizard—if they could die out then there's nothing that could last forever. Everything can change. The continents are moving around, the sea can rise or fall, the stars are changing... and in the English course I have to do, you read about the stuff you speak changing—words, what they mean, the way people can use them to get you to think what they want you to think, talk you into thinking like them, or not thinking at all. You feeling better?

LINDA: Mm.

JENNY: I'm so boring you'd have to cheer up.

LINDA: You're not boring.

JENNY: When's the next pool tournament? No, I want to learn. In the maths course, it's only a general course, Vegie Maths all the smart school kids call it, but I'm doing probability and I was trying to figure out the probability of you winning.

LINDA: And how was it?

JENNY: No way!

SCENE 19

Sam's place.

A)

JANE: Still awake?
SAM: Still working.
JANE: Poetry.
SAM: Ah… yes… umm… John Donne.
JANE: You've started chewing gum.
SAM: Calms me down.
JANE: No problems?
SAM: I don't want to do this exam.
JANE: Then don't do it. It's ridiculous to waste a year of your life worrying about a piece of paper. Forget the exam. Forget school. Take off, go away somewhere and do nothing, just… live. The exam! Forget the exam!

B)

JANE: Still awake?
SAM: Still working.
JANE: Poetry.
SAM: Ah… yes… umm… John Donne.
JANE: You've started chewing gum.
SAM: Calms me down.
JANE: No problems?
SAM: No. I get a bit tired sometimes.
JANE: Is that lamp strong enough? If it's not I can easily get you a better one.
SAM: The lamp's fine.
JANE: Milo?
SAM: Nothing.
JANE: Goodnight.
SAM: Yep.

SCENE 20

Suburban house.

KID: I hope this is the right house. I've been watching it for weeks, but what if she was only visiting someone. No. This must be where she lives. All those photos of her family on the mantelpiece. Now where would a supervisor keep exam papers? Oh no, what if she's got a safe? You idiot, you didn't think of that. Stop. Calm down. Keep the torch down low, what if a neighbour sees? Now this looks like a study. This'll be her desk I bet. Locked, probably. I'm too young to have a credit card, it'd be easy to open. If I shine the torch through the opening—pens, pad, stapler, paper clips... No, much too small for exam papers. What if she's forgotten something and comes back? Right now she's probably turning the car around and heading back down the street. I'm getting out of here. No. Stop. You've come this far. Think about how badly you did in the half-yearly. Think about the marks you got. Think about how two assignments got lousy marks. Remember what your father said when your mother told him you hadn't done as well as expected. And what about promising to do much better in the real thing? How can I? I can't think at all, I'm so nervous all the time. But I have to get a decent mark. Or I've had it. What's this? Old cardigan. But underneath. I can't believe it. She's left them lying here under an old cardigan. English, Mathematics, Industrial Science, French, Biology... all here. Just sitting here in a corner of the room. Great, they weigh a ton. There's a car. No. It's going past. Okay. Here we go. A cardboard box full of success. Torch off. Slowly, slowly...

He goes.

SCENE 21

School hall.
All the candidates line up on chairs. SUPERVISORS *hand out the papers.*

PART TWO

SUPERVISOR: Coooooomm… ence!
KIDS: [*chanting*]
Write your candidate number at the top right-hand corner of the page.
You must not write in red nor mark your page in any way in red.
Answer any two questions. The questions are of equal value.
Read this instruction carefully. Answer three questions only from Part Two.
Answer any two of the following. All questions in Part One are compulsory.

> *They begin writing. Slowly the tapping of their pens creates a rhythm. Individually and in chorus they puzzle over the exam questions. During this, one student drops his or her pen on the floor and the whole room freezes in horror. They all watch the student timidly retrieve the pen. Then a student farts and the smell travels across the entire room.*

Translate into English.
Do the opportunities open to men and women in society differ?
Discuss the main characteristics of Baroque Art.
Explain in detail resistance to disease.
What are the distinctive qualities of Emily Dickinson's poetry?
What material is used to brace roof trusses?
What were the problems of the poor in NSW in the period up to 1850?
To what key does section three modulate?
Give the valency of sulphur in each of the following formulas.
Why is the calculation of Wool Base important in Wool Testing?
Discuss the effects of the Louisiana Purchase.
What is meant by continental drift?
Find all the real numbers for x which satisfy the following equation.
An eclipse of the moon occurs because?
Translate into Polish Slovenian Greek French Estonian Arabic Latin Italian Classical Greek Spanish German Vietnamese Indonesian Japanese *Russian*!

> *They all look at their watches and then gasp in horror at how little time they have left. They scribble furiously, muttering possible answers to themselves.*

SUPERVISOR: Cease writing.

They all scribble more frantically.

Cease writing!

They all put their pens down. The SUPERVISORS *collect the papers. The students all tip-toe from the hall then collapse into roars of relief, anguish, joy and despair.*

SCENE 22

Holiday house.

DANNY: Listen to that sound. The surf pounding away, you can breathe in the spray. In a day, less, we'll have forgotten the exams. Just sun and sand and relaxation. Let's go! Free at last. Let's hit the water.

SAM: You coming?

JANE: No, not yet. You use blockout.

DANNY: The hole in the ozone layer, caused by chlorofluorocarbons emitted from aerosol spraycans and fridges. Result, increased ultraviolet radiation! But let's hit the beach.

SAM and DANNY go.

GRAHAM: Those two boys making friends is the best thing that ever happened. You wouldn't think a kid could change so much.

JANE: No you wouldn't. I've made a decision. I'm not going to pressure Sam into any-thing. I don't know what's happening to him. He's changed too much.

GRAHAM: He's been a bit nervous.

JANE: We're too distant. No result is worth it. Whatever he gets in the exam, he can do what he likes. I'm not going to get my satisfaction out of his hard work. If he wants to do nothing for the next five years, I don't care. Let him.

GRAHAM: I thought he'd decided to go to university.

JANE: But if he doesn't want to, I won't care.

GRAHAM: Won't you?

JANE: Will you push Danny to go on?

SAM comes in, stops and listens.

GRAHAM: I think we should wait for the results. Stop worrying. You like it here?

JANE: It's very peaceful. It makes a. difference seeing the beach from up here. You could jump out the window and be in the surf.

GRAHAM: You could come here more often if you wanted to. On a regular basis.

JANE: Graham, we've been very careful dealing with each other. You did me a favour helping with money. Will you do another one?

GRAHAM: What?

JANE: Just leave things be, for now.

GRAHAM notices SAM.

SAM: Did we bring my flippers?

JANE: I thought you'd gone down to the beach.

SAM: I forgot the flippers.

JANE: They're in the boot, in that old hessian bag.

SAM: Great.

SAM goes.

JANE: Oh no.

GRAHAM: He couldn't have heard.

JANE: This was a mistake, I know it.

GRAHAM: We're here to relax, wind down. Now let's all do that.

SCENE 23

Committal centre.

IAN: This place. What hope would you have once you were sent here? You been in one of these places before?

CATH: I don't know why they have to make us wait. I just want to get this done and move on.

IAN: What are you going to ask about? Anything specific?

CATH: Nothing you need to know about.

IAN: I'm just going to be cut right out of this now?

CATH: We just stick to the jobs we have.

IAN: I never thought you'd be the type to sulk.

CATH: I am not sulking.

IAN: I'd say you were.

CATH: It's only because you're on staff with a contract you're still working on this. I asked for someone less irresponsible but it'd take too long to find a replacement.

IAN: I hate sulkers.

CATH: Ian, I don't care.

IAN: Especially women. Women who want to be treated as equal, do as a good a job as a man, but you try and question something and they behave like women, they sulk, and give you the cold shoulder and dirty looks and try and make you feel guilty. So what are we going to do? A story about convicted criminals being given luxury accommodation and an education? That the angle?

CATH: The people who've seen what we've got so far think it might be a bit soft.

IAN: A few shots of skinheads lounging around the pool doing their lessons. That should do it.

CATH: This is hardly luxury.

IAN: It upset you?

CATH: Yes. I don't know why I thought of coming in here. I hate the atmosphere. I hate the smell.

    JENNY comes in.

JENNY: Hullo. The youth worker said you wanted to talk to me.

CATH: Jenny? I'm… we are talking to all sorts of people involved with the HSC. You're studying while you're here?

JENNY: Yes.

CATH: Would you mind talking? You'll be on TV.

IAN: Don't let that sway you.

JENNY: I don't know what I'd say.

CATH: I'll just ask you a few questions. Okay?

JENNY: Well…

IAN: But you don't have to. Does she? No… you don't.

JENNY: Well, I don't mind, I s'pose.

CATH: Great. Let's start. You right?

IAN: Tape's rolling.

CATH: Interview with Jenny, a prisoner in—

JENNY: A prisoner?

CATH: What should we call you? Inmate?
JENNY: Yuck.
CATH: Well... Interview with Jenny.
JENNY: Will I have a black square over my face?
CATH: What for?
JENNY: Well, when they interview people inside on TV they always have black squares over their faces.
CATH: Do you want that?
JENNY: Then no-one'll know it's me.
CATH: Exactly. Now Jenny—
JENNY: When will it be on?
CATH: We don't actually know yet. Pretty soon though, when the results come out.
JENNY: I don't want to miss it. Linda, my mate, said I absolutely had to find out when it's on.
CATH: We'll let you know. Right. Jenny... some people might be a bit surprised that someone who's been put somewhere like this is studying. Do you think it's right?
JENNY: What?
CATH: That you're in here to be punished and yet you're doing your HSC.
JENNY: But if I don't do it now maybe my whole life'll be a mess. I'm here for a little while, not my whole life.
CATH: Is the exam that important?
JENNY: Isn't it? Everybody says it is.
CATH: Yes they do.

Pause.

JENNY: Yes?
CATH: Ah... um.
IAN: Cath?
CATH: What?
IAN: You right?
CATH: Yes. What subjects are you doing?
JENNY: English, Vegie Maths—that's what some people call it because it's a general course, same with Science. General Studies. Nothing much, but I just want to do it, you know, so I'll have it. If you don't have it you're really at the end of the queue. So everyone says.

CATH: Yes. [*Pause.*] Let's cut it there. Thank you... Julie? Jenny. We'll tell you when it's going to be on.

She goes.

JENNY: Is she alright?

IAN: Yes. She's overworked. Good luck with your results.

SCENE 24

Beach.

DANNY: We should go. Tea'll be ready. I'm not going to eat anything tonight. Bet I don't sleep either. I feel so nervous. I didn't feel this nervous doing the exams and it's too late now. I wonder if the postman gets nervous knowing he has to deliver all those results.

SAM: I don't think he'd care all that much.

DANNY: I wonder if people open them and get upset if they haven't done well and attack the postman. Be worse than getting attacked by a dog, wouldn't it?

SAM: Danny...

DANNY: I can't help it. I'm so nervous about tomorrow! Are you?

SAM: Yeah.

DANNY: You don't seem nervous. You seem really calm. Ever since we came up here you've been so quiet. Do you hate it here? Do you hate staying at our place? Would you rather have got your results on your own?

SAM: No.

DANNY: Well what?

SAM: It's not just us who's done the exam. The teachers, all the people with the jobs waiting to see how we went, the universities, the colleges. The parents. This year has gone so quickly. Do you think you're the same person?

DANNY: No.

SAM: I'm not. I can't remember who that person was sitting on the beach that day reading a science fiction book. I've got a terrible headache.

DANNY: Do you really reckon you did okay in the exam?

PART TWO

SAM: I don't know. I don't remember. It was like a dream, the whole thing. I remember the questions, I don't remember what I wrote, nothing. You did well I bet.

DANNY: I bet I did real well. Fantastically well. Better than anyone could believe.

SCENE 25

Committal centre.

LINDA: Are you going to walk around all night?

JENNY: No.

LINDA: How am I supposed to get to sleep?

JENNY: Sorry.

LINDA: There's nothing you can do now so get into bed.

JENNY: I wasn't this upset the night before my hearing. That was nothing compared to this.

LINDA: Look, I've put up with you studying and worrying for a whole year. The least you can do is let us both get a good night's sleep.

JENNY: Yes.

LINDA: I'll call a youth worker. They'll make you settle down.

JENNY: Do you know what time the post actually arrives?

LINDA: Jennifer!

JENNY: I'll go to sleep. Right. I'm in bed and I'm falling asleep. [*She lies there for a while.*] I'm not thinking about the results. [*Pause.*] Or the work I did.

  LINDA *sits up and watches her.*

Or what I'll do if I don't pass. [*Pause.*] Or the whole year that's passed like a minute.

SCENE 26

Studio.

CATH: This is a long night for those fifty-five thousand five hundred and thirty-five young men and women waiting to hear what the future has in store. How many restless minds are lying awake across the state, the country, for that coded list of results that will determine the course of their lives? As the hours until the post arrives slowly tick by, so many hopes, so many ambitions… Um… Shit.

IAN: [*offstage*] You're tired.

CATH: I'm fine.

IAN: [*coming onstage*] You want to go again?

CATH: Yes. No. I'm tired.

IAN: We can pick it up tomorrow.

CATH: We've got to be up early as it is. The post gets out pretty quickly in some suburbs. I suddenly feel completely exhausted. It must be terrible waiting for something in the mail that decides your future.

IAN: We all did it.

CATH: No, I didn't. I didn't do the HSC. I fooled around a lot when I was younger, no discipline all the reports said. Uncontrollable the worst one said. God, I hated school. I had so much energy and I had to keep it in all the time. It was like… it was like a prison. And when I was finally sent to remand centre I found out about real prisons. I came so close to staying in them for the rest of my life. Once I needed money so badly I got a job on a country newspaper bluffing my way in with the worst School Certificate pass ever given. I've been battling my onward and upward ever since. But in that… place we went to. I remembered how close I came. That girl… I couldn't ask a single crummy question. I just wanted to tell her to try. To keep trying and not give in.

IAN: I don't think she will.

CATH: Let's try to record this again.

IAN: Now?

CATH: Yes.

IAN: You're the boss, boss.

CATH: This is a long night for those fifty-five thousand five hundred and thirty-five young men and women waiting to hear what the future has in store. Tomorrow, the envelopes with marks and placings will arrive that will tell students where on society's ladder they are. But are marks, decile ratings, aggregates and so on, all the exam is made up of? The Higher School Certificate is more than an exam. It is a trial by ordeal, by fire, forced on students by a society that demands a rigid coding of ability that leaves little room for creativity, experiment or the varied life experiences of the people actually doing the exam. Achievement occurs not through the exam, but despite it. The marks themselves mean little beside the enormous personal and community upheaval symbolised by those three ominous letters: HSC. It is to all those who pass through this upheaval, no matter their results on paper that this program is dedicated. Cut.

IAN: Boss.
CATH: What?
IAN: Wow.

SCENE 27

A whistle blows and the POSTMAN *delivers results to everyone. At the same time the air is filled with envelopes marked 'Pass' or 'Fail'.*

SCENE 28

Committal centre.

The POSTMAN *brings a letter to* JENNY. *She opens it. She reads it over and over, it seems for hours.*

LINDA: Jen? Well?
JENNY: Two hundred and seventy-six.

    LINDA *shrugs, not understanding.*

I got it.
LINDA: You got it?
JENNY: Yep.
LINDA: You got it! *You got it!*

> *They leap around screaming and laughing, then stop and stare at each other a moment, then throw their arms around each other. They run off and* LINDA *can be heard telling everyone in the place.*

She got it!

SCENE 29

Holiday house.

DANNY: You go first.
SAM: You want to open them?
JANE: No Sam. You open them.

    SAM *opens the envelope and reads quietly.*

SAM: Four hundred and thirty-eight.
DANNY: Four hundred and thirty-eight?
SAM: Yes. Four hundred and thirty-eight. Now you.

    DANNY *opens his envelope.*

DANNY: Oh dear.
GRAHAM: What did you get?
DANNY: Oh dear. It's not good.
GRAHAM: What do you mean it's not good? Give it to me.
DANNY: You won't like it.
GRAHAM: You failed. You failed everything.
JANE: Oh, Danny, no, that's terrible.
SAM: You failed?
JANE: It's a mistake, it has to be.
GRAHAM: It's ridiculous. Who do you ring? The Education Department, I suppose.
DANNY: Sorry. It's not a mistake.
GRAHAM: You can't have failed. It's not possible. You improved so much. Your assess-ments were good. The teachers said you'd do well. You worked hard.
DANNY: They couldn't really give a mark to blank paper though, could they?
SAM: You didn't.
GRAHAM: Blank paper…
DANNY: I just stared at the page until they made us stop work. I just handed the blank booklets in again at the end. All they had on them was my name and the name of the exam. So they couldn't really give me a mark, could they?

GRAHAM: What have you done?
DANNY: Sorry.
GRAHAM: Sorry? I can't believe this.
DANNY: Thank you for all your help.
SAM: You should have passed. After all that…
GRAHAM: I hope you're pleased with yourself.
DANNY: No.
SAM: I wish I hadn't passed. I should have done the same.
JANE: You don't ever have to put yourself through anything like that again. You can do nothing. I won't care. I won't ever force you to do anything ever again.
GRAHAM: You haven't.
JANE: I've forced him, very gently, but I've forced him. No more.
GRAHAM: He's going to university.
JANE: If he wants to.
GRAHAM: It's been decided.
JANE: It's been assumed.
GRAHAM: That's fine for you to say. What have I been putting money into then?
JANE: I don't know, what have you been putting money into? I thought it was friendship.
GRAHAM: Sure. But I want to see something for it. I wasn't offering to throw it away.
JANE: Suddenly this house feels completely different. That beach feels completely different. I think we should go, first thing in the morning.
GRAHAM: You can't leave, just like that. I want to hear Sam discuss his future. I have a right. I helped him with his future, I have a stake in it.
JANE: Yes I suppose you do, looking at it from your point of view.
GRAHAM: I'm not going to cut off a pound of flesh.
JANE: You want a kid's future. That's much worse.
DANNY: Oh, stop yelling.
JANE: Sam. I need some air.

    SAM *and* JANE *go.*

DANNY: What have you been putting money into?
GRAHAM: You wouldn't understand.

DANNY: A new kid? Were you investing in a new kid?

GRAHAM: Since you started improving at school I never thought of it like that. Some-thing else made me do it. I like being with her. I like to have her around. I like to help her when she needs it. I thought maybe I had it made.

DANNY: I stuffed it right up.

GRAHAM: You just sat there, all through those exams?

DANNY: The time went so slowly.

GRAHAM: What were you thinking?

DANNY: I was thinking about the day I met Sam on the beach and after he'd gone you told me that life was going to get narrower or something. I sat there all through those exams trying to feel my life getting narrower. It was amazing. My heart kept pounding, any second I could have picked up the pen and written like crazy and got something. I had complete control over my whole life. So I made myself sit there and colour in the O's with the pen. And then they'd say 'Cease writing' and it would be over again. And when the last exam was finished it was like the curtain closing when the movie's over. The End. So now my life is narrow. I'm free. I got to learn a few things. That's what education's for.

SCENE 30

Eastern suburbs living room.

CATH: I suppose congratulations are in order.

STUDENT: Thank you.

CATH: Do you think you deserved to come top of the state?

STUDENT: Yes.

CATH: You worked hard for it then?

STUDENT: Of course I did.

CATH: You must be very proud of your son.

MOTHER: Yes, this is a very happy day.

STUDENT: Actually I'm not all that pleased. I know I got four hundred and ninety-eight marks out of a possible five hundred, but I really feel I should have done better. I'm going to appeal.

CATH: Appeal?! I mean, why are you going to appeal?

STUDENT: There was a slight prejudice against someone doing the subjects I chose. Allowance should really have been made. If the marking were done fairly I would have got four hundred and ninety-nine. I think it's appalling, very unfair.
MOTHER: It's really rather poor, don't you think?
CATH: And what are you going to do with this top mark?
STUDENT: Well, it's difficult to say really. They really want me at medical school, they're practically begging for me to enrol there, but I don't know, merchant banking looks rather attractive too. It depends which possible career has the highest potential in the end.
CATH: Of course. And how do you all intend to celebrate this success?
MOTHER: Well, we've got some lovely French champagne on ice, just waiting to be opened.
STUDENT: And Dad's sending me to the Maldives as a congratulations present. I'm not sure if I'll go yet because I don't want to miss the enrolment dates for the universities. I'm just waiting to see if I'd have access to a fax there.
CATH: Thank you very much. Cut.
MOTHER: Won't you stay and have a glass with us?
CATH: Ian?
IAN: No, I have to go outside to be sick. Thanks anyway.
CATH: And I never drink with dickheads. I make it a rule. Goodbye.

SCENE 31

Beach.

SAM: I was sitting here reading something, nothing to do with school and Danny just came straight up and started talking. A year ago.
JANE: Sam…
SAM: Yes.
JANE: I don't know.
SAM: No, say it. Say what you wanted to say.
JANE: You're like a stranger to me.
SAM: I feel like a stranger.
JANE: I don't know how we got through that year.
SAM: It was very lonely.

JANE: Yes it was.
SAM: Do you actually like him?
JANE: Yes I do.
SAM: Not because you have to?
JANE: Sam…
SAM: No, say it. Say what you really want to say.
JANE: He's been very good to me. He's helped me.
SAM: Not just with money?
JANE: You don't understand everything—
SAM: Doesn't matter, just keep saying what you really think. All the times we've been on the edge of saying what we really want, too scared to just let go and jump.
JANE: I've never felt more confused in my life. Nothing's gone the way I wanted it to. He never took advantage of me. He has been like a very good friend. If I'm really honest, yes I looked forward to seeing him again. I think he would say the same.
SAM: But the things he said—
JANE: Danny's results.
SAM: He doesn't really think like that?
JANE: I hope not. I don't want to lose his friendship. But…
SAM: No, go on.
JANE: I'm afraid I've lost you.
SAM: I was afraid your whole life depended on me.
JANE: I'm sorry.
SAM: And now. It's a holiday. We're lucky, aren't we?
JANE: Yes.
SAM: Won't be much of a holiday for Danny and his father.
JANE: It's going to be very difficult.
SAM: They won't even be able to talk to each other.
JANE: Maybe we can teach them.

THE END